SOCCER BIOGRAPHIES

KYLIAN MBAPPÉ

KENNY ABDO

Fly!
An Imprint of Abdo Zoom
abdobooks.com

abdobooks.com

Published by Abdo Zoom, a division of ABDO, P.O. Box 398166, Minneapolis, Minnesota 55439.

Printed in China.
052025
092025

THIS BOOK CONTAINS RECYCLED MATERIALS

Photo Credits: Alamy, AP Images, Getty Images, Icon Sportwire, Shutterstock
Production Contributors: Kenny Abdo, Jennie Forsberg, Grace Hansen
Design Contributors: Candice Keimig, Neil Klinepier, Victoria Bates

Library of Congress Control Number: 2024947819

Publisher's Cataloging-in-Publication Data

Names: Abdo, Kenny, author.
Title: Kylian Mbappé / by Kenny Abdo
Description: Minneapolis, Minnesota : Abdo Zoom, 2026 | Series: Soccer biographies | Includes online resources and index.
Identifiers: ISBN 9781098288853 (lib. bdg.) | ISBN 9781098289553 (ebook) | ISBN 9781098289904 (Read-to-me ebook)
Subjects: LCSH: Mbappé, Kylian, 1998---Juvenile literature. | Soccer players--Biography--Juvenile literature. | Professional athletes--Biography--Juvenile literature. | La Liga (Soccer league)--Juvenile literature.
Classification: DDC 796.334092--dc23

TABLE OF CONTENTS

KYLIAN MBAPPÉ

Kylian Mbappé has sprinted his way to the top as one of the best soccer players in the world, proving he's a real goal-getter!

Fly
29
PARIS

EARLY YEARS

Mbappé was born in 1998 in Bondy, France. He showed massive talent for soccer early on. His parents **encouraged** him to follow his passion. As a child, Mbappé often played street soccer and practiced in local parks. His speed and skill quickly caught people's attention.

A.J.AUXERRE
CENTRE DE FORMATION
A.J.AUXERRE
ACADOMIA
AJ AUXERRE

Mbappé was accepted to the respected Clairefontaine Academy. The 12-year-old quickly stood out as one of its best players. By 2013, AS Monaco had signed the 14-year-old. Mbappé broke many records with the team.

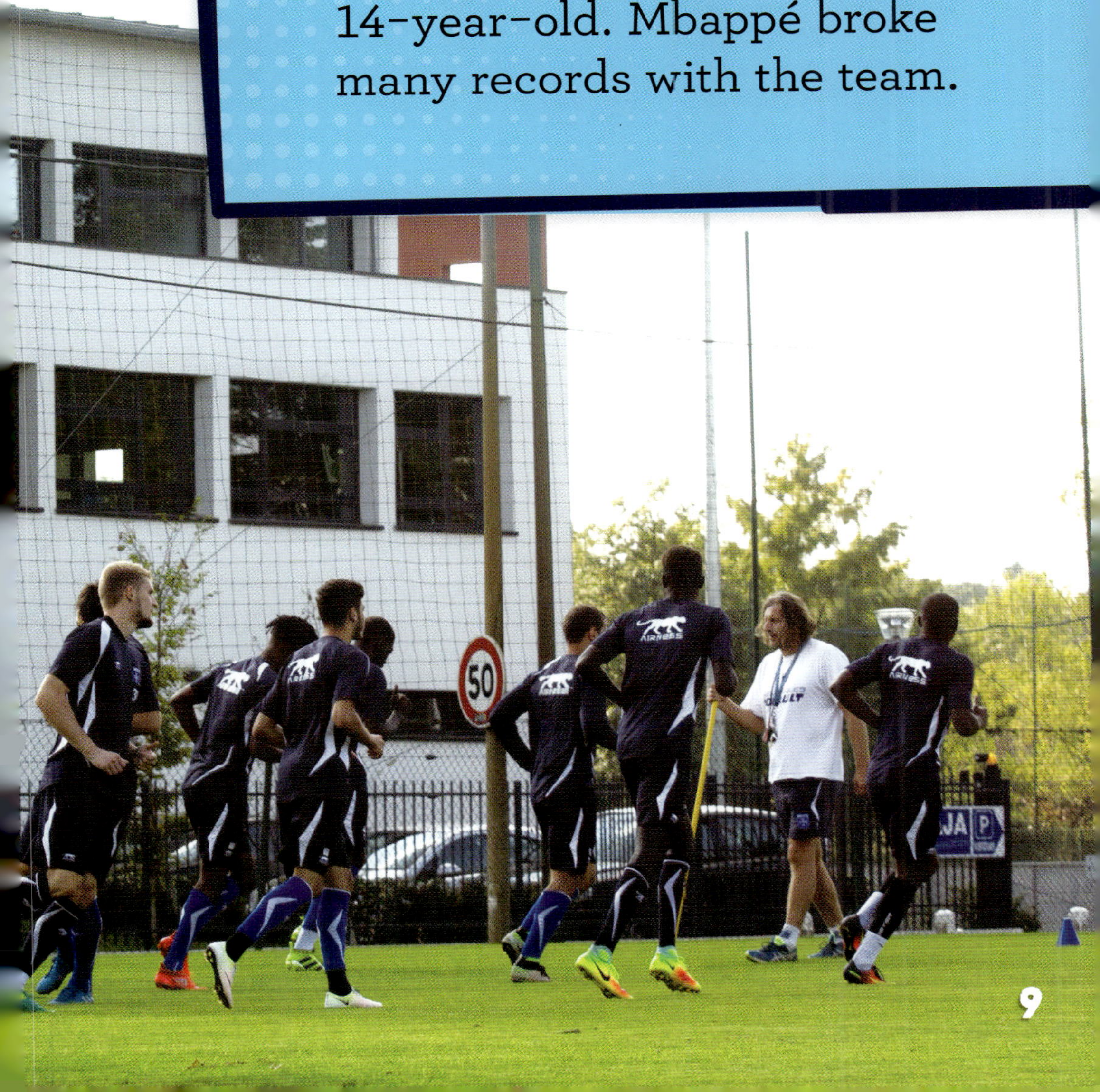

GOING PRO

During the 2016–17 season, Mbappé helped Monaco win the **Ligue 1** title! He ended the season with 26 goals in 44 matches. Mbappé was also named Ligue 1 Young Player of the Year!

Mbappé joined Paris Saint-Germain (PSG) in 2017. He helped the team win the **Ligue 1** title during the 2017–18 season. PSG was named the **UEFA** Team of the Year. Mbappé also won the 2018 Kopa Trophy. It is an award given to the best under-21 player in the world.

UP™ FINAL 2018

FIFA

That same year, Mbappé helped nab a **World Cup** victory. He became the youngest French player to score four goals during the tournament! Mbappé received the **FIFA World Cup** Best Young Player award for his performance.

Fly
Emirates

In the 2018–19 season, Mbappé scored 33 goals in **Ligue 1**. He was honored with the French Player of the Year award. Mbappé's skills helped PSG in securing another league title!

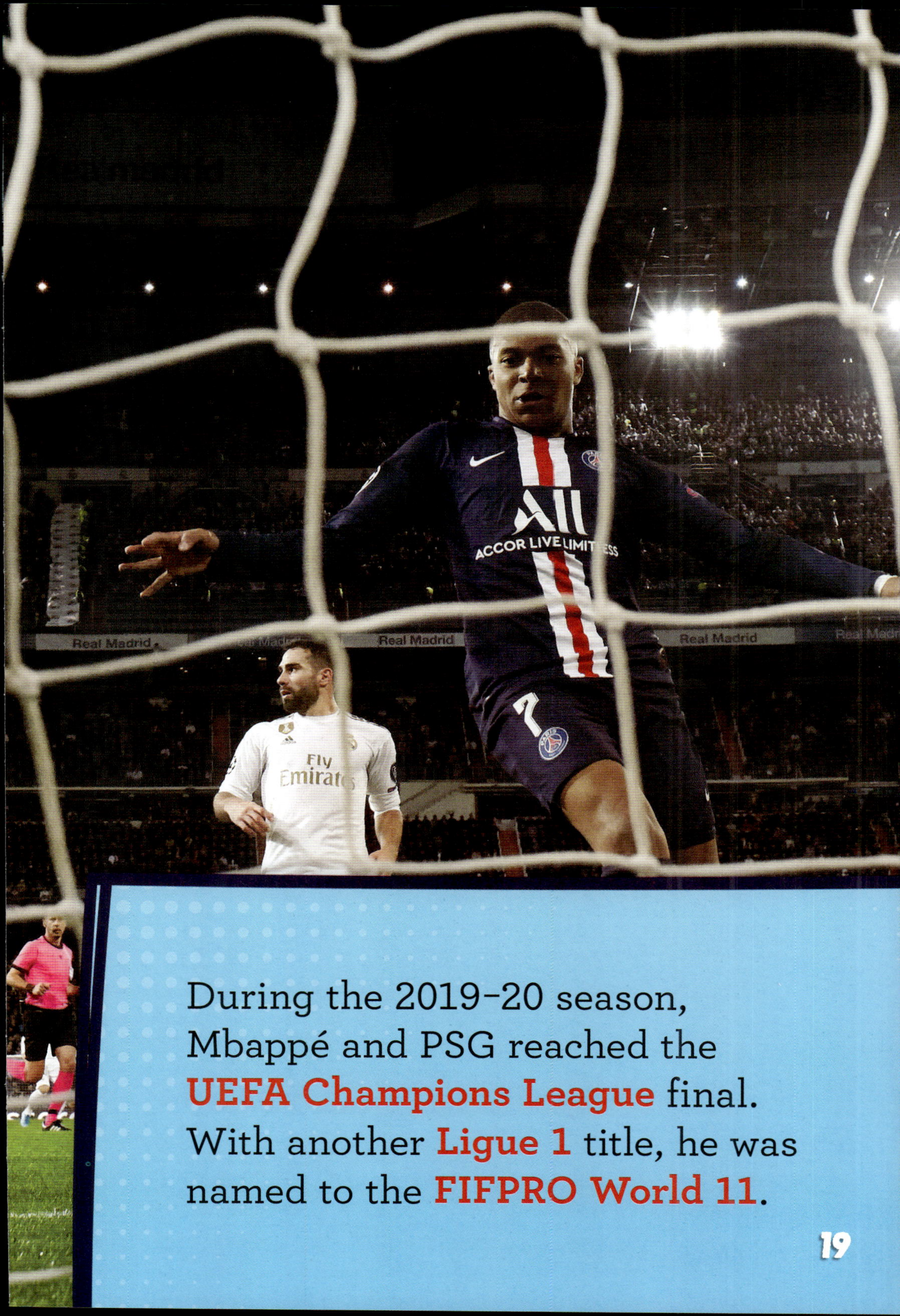

During the 2019–20 season, Mbappé and PSG reached the **UEFA Champions League** final. With another **Ligue 1** title, he was named to the **FIFPRO World 11**.

Mbappé was the top scorer in the French league during the 2020–21 season. He helped the team reach the **Champions League** semifinals! He also secured another **Ligue 1** title. Mbappé capped off the 2022 season with a **Golden Boot** trophy after leading the team to another **World Cup** final!

10
FIFA World Cup Qatar 2022
DEN BOOT AW

QATAR
AIRWAYS

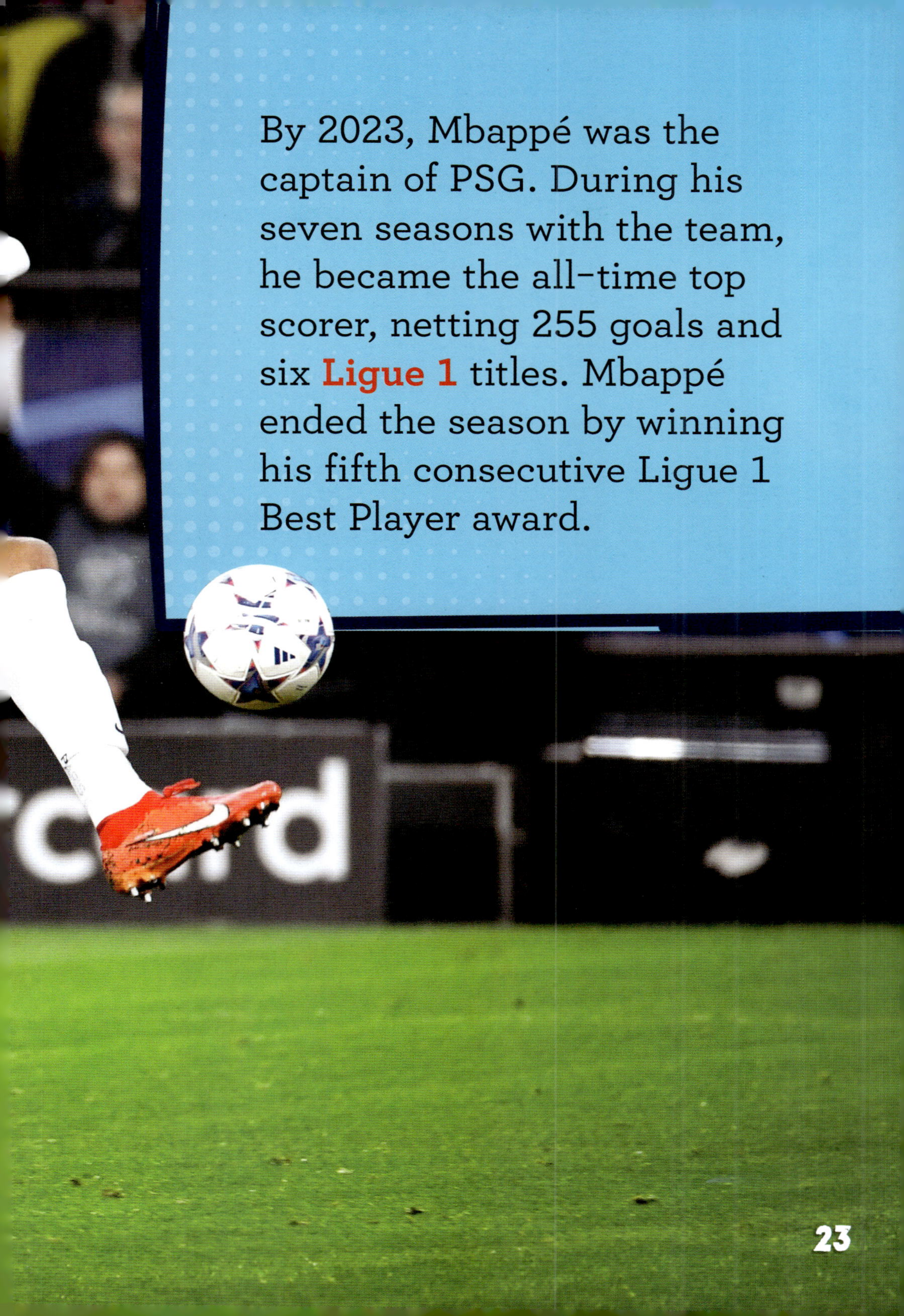

By 2023, Mbappé was the captain of PSG. During his seven seasons with the team, he became the all-time top scorer, netting 255 goals and six **Ligue 1** titles. Mbappé ended the season by winning his fifth consecutive Ligue 1 Best Player award.

In 2024, Mbappé left PSG for Real Madrid. He impressed fans old and new by helping his new team win the **Spanish Super Cup** against Atalanta BC!

WINNERS
UEFA SUPER CUP 2024

LEGACY

Off the field, Mbappé uses his skills to inspire kids. He supports organizations like Premiers de Cordée, which offers free sports activities to children with disabilities. Mbappé is also the **ambassador** for the organic brand Good Goût Kidz!

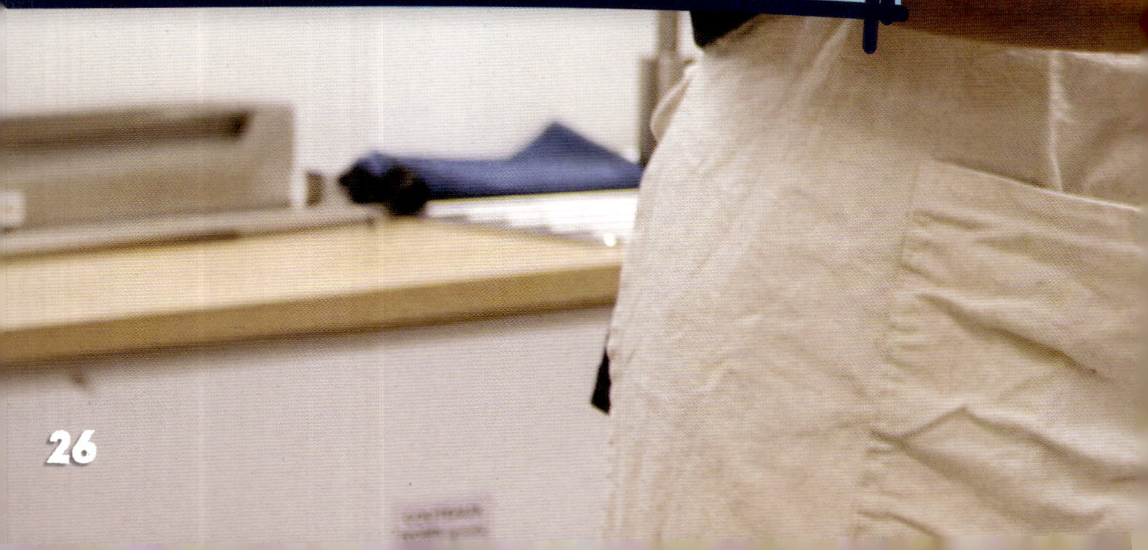

GoodPlast

Mbappé's career has seen many records broken and awards earned. He remains one of soccer's most exciting figures because he's always kicking it up a notch!

MBAPPÉ
7

GLOSSARY

ambassador – anyone who is sent as a representative or messenger.

Champions League – a yearly soccer competition organized by the UEFA.

encouraged – gave hope or support to.

FIFA – the international organization for men's and women's soccer.

FIFPRO World 11 – a yearly award given to the best soccer players currently active, voted on by the players themselves.

Golden Boot – an award given to the league's top goal scorers each season.

Ligue 1 – the top soccer league in France. It has 18 teams that can move up to or down from Ligue 2.

Spanish Super Cup – a yearly soccer game between the Champions League and UEFA Europa League winners.

World Cup – an international soccer competition held every four years.

UEFA – short for Union of European Football Associations.

ONLINE RESOURCES

Booklinks
NONFICTION NETWORK
FREE! ONLINE NONFICTION RESOURCES

To learn more about Kylian Mbappé, please visit **abdobooklinks.com** or scan this QR code. These links are routinely monitored and updated to provide the most current information available.

INDEX